Pet Care Prowess
Establishing Your Own Pet Sitting and Dog Walking Business

Table of Contents

Chapter 1. Introduction

Unleash your passion for pets and channel that fervor into a thriving pet care business through our Special Report: "Pet Care Prowess: Establishing Your Own Pet Sitting and Dog Walking Business". With a cheerful, enthusiastic, and informative approach, we aim to guide animal lovers like you in turning your passion into a profitable venture successfully. This comprehensive guide outlines every tiny detail from the basics of startup strategies, to deep dives into industry insights, marketing efforts, legal requirements, financial planning, and much more. Whether you are already into pet care services or are an absolute beginner, this report is sure to kindle the entrepreneurial spirit within you. So why wait? Start your journey towards 'petrepreneurship' today, and establish your pet sitting and dog walking business with panache and prowess. Buckle up for an exciting, fulfilling, and prosperous pet care adventure!

Chapter 2. Unleashing the Potential: A Primer in Pet Care Business

There's a petal-strewn path that awaits you where you get to work with your favorite creatures every day: your dream-turned-reality pet care business. Dogs, cats, fish, birds: there are pet owners aplenty who could benefit from your attentive services. But where do you begin in turning this passion into a real, money-making enterprise? Let's take a closer look.

2.1. The Pet Care Landscape

The pet care industry is continually expanding, estimated to be worth over $100 billion in the U.S. alone. More than just simple economics, the emotional connection between humans and pets is the backbone of this booming sector. Understanding that affectionate bond helps to gauge the vast potential that comes with offering pet care services.

For prosperity and growth in this arena, a thorough understanding of the market, the consumers (both the pets and their owners), the geographical area of operation, and the existing competition is crucial. The pet industry segment consists largely of pet food, veterinary care, supplies, over-the-counter medicines, live animal purchases, and grooming & boarding. Your focus will primarily be on the grooming & boarding aspect, which allows room to diversify into dog walking, pet sitting, and even pet transportation.

2.2. Starting Up the Dream Machine

Before you can start providing services, you need a plan – a business plan. This strategy is your road map, outlining advantages, utilities, financial predictions, marketing strategies, and an operational plan. Consider including services like pet sitting, dog walking, pet grooming, pet transportation, and pet training into the mix depending on your competence, comfort, and the local demand.

Your plan should pivot on the following points:

- Service list and pricing
- Target market and consumer profiling
- Marketing and customer acquisition plans
- Operational and organizational structure
- Risk analysis and mitigation strategies
- Financial predictions, budgeting, and proposed funds sourcing

2.3. Becoming Familiar with Furry Friends

Being comfortable with various types of pets and understanding their needs is paramount. Information about different breeds, common pet illnesses, dietary requirements, behavioural aspects, and basic first aid could be crucial. You don't necessarily need to be a vet, but you should know when to call one. Consider taking pet handling and care courses, and maybe even first aid classes.

2.4. The Legalities

Start your business on the right paw with appropriate legal protection. In the U.S., pet care businesses often operate as sole proprietorships or LLCs. Each option has certain legal and financial implications. Research the right fit for you and register your business with the necessary entities. Also, consider obtaining the right insurances. General liability, professional liability, and workers' compensation are primary coverages to consider. Remember, insurance not only protects you but also builds trust with your customers.

2.5. Location Location Location

In many cases, a pet care business requires minimal or often zero infrastructure, as most services are performed at the client's house or during walks. But in some cases, a storefront or office site might be beneficial to provide grooming services, conduct consultations, and meet clients. Location is key, so scout out a spot in a populated area with a high density of pet owners.

2.6. Honing Your Marketing Strategy

Without effective marketing, even the best businesses remain unknown. Advertising your services effectively brings your business to the attention of potential clients. This can include online strategies like SEO, social media marketing, content marketing, and Google AdWords, along with traditional marketing methods. Don't forget word-of-mouth; satisfied clients are your best brand ambassadors.

2.7. Finances and Charging For Your Services

Understanding your expenses and predicting potential income is key to stabilizing and growing your business. Calculate operational costs, and price your services competitively but also economically viable. Start-up costs can be still low for a pet care business, but be sure to account for any needed insurance, licensing, marketing, and possible location rental.

Establishing your own pet care business might seem daunting at first glance, but by taking methodical, careful steps, you can set yourself up for long-term success. Remember that above all else, your love for animals and dedication to their care is your primary motivation. Budgets, spreadsheets, marketing plans – these elements are merely tools to help you turn your passion into your career. Give yourself time to grow and learn, and don't be disheartened by initial challenges. Your love for pets can indeed become the prosperous pet care venture you envision.

Chapter 3. Creating Your Unique Business Proposition

In crafting a unique business proposition, it's crucial to examine certain aspects of your intended pet care business that can set you apart from the competition. A compelling unique business proposition is what can ignite customers' interest and evoke loyalty while distinguishing you from competitors.

3.1. Identifying Your Audience

Your first step in creating a unique business proposition is identifying your target audience. Demographics, pet ownership patterns, their needs, and lifestyle can play an integral role while defining your audience. A well-known fact is that Millennials, more than any other demographic, are significant drivers of the pet industry. Studies have shown that Millennials are willing to spend more on pet care, often viewing their pets as family.

3.2. Defining Your Services

Next, define what services you'll offer. These could range from basic pet sitting and dog walking to more specialized services like pet grooming, health check-ups, and training. Consider offering value-added services such as pet taxi or pick up and drop off, in-home care, overnight stays, or emergency vet visit support. These services can significantly distinguish your business from others.

3.3. Analyzing Your Competition

Now, turn your attention to your competitors. Study local and national service providers alike. Analyze them to understand their strengths, weaknesses, unique selling points, pricing, and operational procedures. This analysis will not only tell you what's already out there but also identify gaps in the market where you could potentially offer something different.

3.4. Unique Selling Proposition

After analyzing your competition, use the insights gained to develop your unique selling proposition (USP). Your USP could be anything from tours of your facilities that demonstrate your commitment to cleanliness and safety, certifications from recognized pet care institutions, special add-ons you provide, or even things like eco-friendly operations. Remember, your USP should be compelling enough to spark interest and make potential customers choose you over others.

3.5. Operational Excellence

Select hours that best serve your clientele. Pet owners often need support outside of traditional working hours, so consider offering services on evenings, weekends, and holidays. Show your commitment to maintaining a high degree of professionalism at all times, from first contact to final service delivery. Always deliver your services on time, and ensure you communicate effectively with your clients.

3.6. Pricing Strategy

Your pricing structure should reflect the value you provide. Higher prices can be justified by exemplary services, unique features, or additional conveniences. On the other hand, if you decide to compete on price, ensure that your business model is sustainable and profitable.

3.7. Customer Service

It's essential to build great relationships with your clients. Stellar customer service can be a vital part of your unique business proposition. Be approachable, be empathetic, and always go the extra mile. High levels of customer satisfaction can lead to repeat business and word-of-mouth referrals.

3.8. Leveraging Technology

Consider leveraging technology in your pet care business. An app or website that facilitates online scheduling, appointment reminders, pet health tracking, online payment, reviews, and feedback can add significant value to your offerings.

3.9. Setting Industry Standards

Strive to be the gold standard in your local pet care industry. Use your unique business proposition as a platform to develop an overarching brand. Train your staff not only in pet care but in customer service and business protocol as well. Be a leader, and let that ethos permeate every aspect of your business.

Creating a unique business proposition is not a one-and-done task. It's a continuous process that involves listening to your customers, constant innovation, and improvements. Remember, you don't just want to offer pet sitting and dog walking services; you want to provide 'pet care excellence'. Let that guide your journey as you carve out your unique place in the fast-growing pet care industry.

Chapter 4. The A-Z of Pet Care Services

Understanding the vast universe of pet care services is the foundation upon which you can build a successful business. This comprehensive guide will sketch out every single aspect for you, from the most basic pet care services to the intricate responsibilities every 'petrepreneur' should be aware of. It's designed to take you on an exhaustive journey through the entire A-Z of pet care services, providing in-depth knowledge and insights, setting the stage for a successful pet care venture.

4.1. The Basics: Dog Walking and Pet Sitting

The heart of most pet care services revolves around two primary basics: dog walking and pet sitting. These are the initial services that most pet service businesses offer.

Dog walking, as it implies, involves taking dogs out for walks, providing them with much-needed exercise and companionship. However, being a successful dog walker doesn't just mean taking a leash and heading off; it comprises understanding the dog's behavior, being aware of safety protocols, and maintaining records of each walk.

Pet sitting, on the other hand, refers to the temporary care given to pets when their guardians are away. Responsibilities might include feeding, grooming, exercising them, and sometimes even administering medication. It's essentially about substitishing the pet's family in their absence and ensuring all their needs are met.

4.2. Special Services: Grooming and Training

Once you have a solid footing in basic services, you might consider expanding into grooming and training.

Grooming a pet isn't solely about keeping them clean, but also about their health and happiness. A professional pet groomer has knowledge about various breeds and their unique needs, the right tools, and an understanding of how to handle distressed animals.

Training is another potential area wherein you teach skills or behaviors to pets. This could range from basic obedience commands with dogs, socializing kittens to litter training rabbits. A background in animal behavior is often useful in enhancing training effectiveness and pet communication.

4.3. Unique Services: Pet Taxi, House Sitting and More

As your business flourishes, you could start offering distinct services, setting you apart from competitors.

A pet taxi service entails transporting pets to their vet appointments or grooming spa wherever their owners cannot.

House sitting combines pet sitting with basic house care services. It includes general tasks like watering plants, managing mail, and maintaining home security, making the service appealing to those who travel frequently.

4.4. Diving Deeper: Health and Wellness Services

Health and wellness services for pets encompass a broader range of services. These could include pet massage, physiotherapy, acupuncture, and even dietary consulting. While these services need specialized training and qualifications, they are highly rewarding and add substantial value to your pet care business.

4.5. Pet Related Products

Selling pet related products, like food, toys, or grooming kits, could be another avenue to explore. By offering products directly from your website or via your office, customers benefit from the convenience, giving them one more reason to choose your services.

4.6. The Bottom Line

This completes the overview of the array of pet care services you can provide. However, each service is a world in itself, filled with unique challenges and rewards. Your passion and dedication as a pet lover, coupled with a thorough understanding of these services, will serve as the beacon propelling your venture towards success. Happy 'petrepreneurship' journey!

(Note: Content is cut short to accommodate general query standards)

Chapter 5. Setting Up Shop: Legal Considerations and Essentials

Before you leap headlong into your pet care business adventure, there are innumerable legal considerations that you need to focus on for a smooth and secure entrepreneurial journey. Tackling these issues upfront is crucial to avoid future headaches and ensure the successful continuity of your pet sitting and dog walking business.

5.1. Understanding Business Structures

Firstly, you must decide the type of business entity that suits your venture. There are various structures to choose from, each with its benefits and drawbacks:

1. Sole Proprietorship
2. Partnership
3. Limited Liability Company (LLC)
4. Corporation

As a sole proprietor, you have complete control over your business, but you also shoulder all the liability. A partnership involves shared ownership, while an LLC separates your personal assets from your business. A corporation is a legal entity separate from its owners, providing maximum protection against personal liability but requires extensive record-keeping, operational processes, and reporting.

Don't rush into a decision; consult a business advisor or attorney to help you evaluate the appropriate structure for your business, considering factors like liability, taxation, and administrative requirements.

5.2. Obtaining Business Licenses and Permits

Depending on your location and the nature of services you offer, you may require specific business licenses and permits. These can include a general business license, a professional or occupational license, a health permit, or a sign permit. Reach out to local authorities or a business counselor for details about necessary permits in your area.

5.3. Getting Insured

Purchasing the right insurance is key to protecting your business from liability and unexpected incidents. The primary types of insurance for pet care businesses include:

1. General Liability Insurance
2. Animal Bailee Insurance
3. Workers' Compensation Insurance
4. Commercial Auto Insurance

General liability insurance offers coverage for bodily or personal injury, property damage, or advertising injury. Animal Bailee insurance protects you if a pet is lost, injured, or passes away under your care. If you hire employees, workers' compensation insurance becomes critical to protect your business from lawsuits. If your business involves transportation, commercial auto insurance covers property damage and medical expenses in case of accidents.

5.4. Contract and Legal Documentation

It's always smart to have written agreements in place between you and your clients. Your contract should clearly state the services you provide, the fees, cancellation policy, emergency procedures and liability issues.

Other vital documents include a service agreement, veterinary release form, and photo release form if you plan to take pictures of the pets for business promotion.

5.5. Animal Welfare Acts, Regulations, and Compliance

Ensure compliance with any regional animal welfare acts, regulations and standards. Regulations can include vaccination requirements, pet handling procedures, and safety regulations.

5.6. Trademark, Copyright, and Intellectual Property

Lastly, consider registering your business name and logo as trademarks to protect them from being used by competitors.

This chapter has laid the groundwork for the legal aspects to consider when setting up your pet sitting and dog walking business. Getting the basics in place will provide a solid foundation for your venture. Your disregard of or non-compliance with these legal requirements could lead to penal ramifications, which might even cause business discontinuity. Therefore, it's always better to get these things straight right at the outset to ensure a secure and smoother journey in your entrepreneurial endeavor.

Always remember, investing time and effort in the initial stages to comply with legal necessities is a priceless investment that could save immense troubles in the future. With these legal considerations and essentials sincerely addressed and tactfully handled, you are one step closer to becoming a successful 'petrepreneur'!

Chapter 6. Marketing Your Furry Business: Planning and Strategies

A robust marketing strategy is essential to establish and expand any business, particularly when it comes to pet care. While your proficiency in handling various pets will certainly attract clientele, the way you present your services to potential customers will either make or break your enterprise. With the right knowledge and tools, you can optimize your marketing efforts to not only increase awareness about your business but also foster trust among the pet parents.

6.1. Understanding Your Market

Before you start planning your marketing, it is vital to comprehend the market you are entering. Conducting a thorough market analysis is crucial to understanding the needs and wants of your potential customers.

Researching the pet care industry and understanding its nuances can reveal substantial insight into the pet parents' minds. Ask the following questions:

- What kind of pets are common in your area?

- What pet care services are heavily in demand?

- What are the strategies that successful pet care businesses have used?

- Who are your competitors and how do they market their services?

Make a note of your findings, as these will help you develop an insightful, impactful, and strategic marketing plan.

6.2. Identifying Your Unique Selling Proposition (USP)

In a market crowded with similar services, what sets you apart? Your Unique Selling Proposition (USP) is that unique feature or benefit that differentiates your pet care service from others.

It could be your years of experience, specialized training, pet-friendly amenities, or even your exceptional customer service. Identify your USP and ensure it is at the heart of your marketing messages.

6.3. Defining Your Target Audience

Defining who you want to reach with your marketing efforts is essential. Your target audience should encompass pet owners that resonate with your USP.

Your target clientele might be working professionals, senior citizens, households with kids, etc., depending on the services you provide. Each group has different needs and will respond to different types of messaging.

6.4. Crafting Your Message

Now that you know what sets you apart and whom you're targeting, it's time to craft a compelling message. The goal is to inform potential clients about your business, engage them and inspire them to choose your pet care services.

Make sure to highlight what's special about your services, why they should trust you with their beloved pets, and how you can add value to their lives.

6.5. Choosing the Right Channels

The selection of the right promotional channels is key to reaching your target audience. The choice of platforms will depend on where your target audience is likely to spend their time.

Consider these platforms:

- Community bulletin boards
- Local newspapers or newsletters
- Social media channels like Facebook, Instagram, or TikTok
- Your business website
- E-mail newsletters

Identify which platforms are best for reaching your desired audience, then focus your efforts on those channels.

6.6. Social Media Marketing

In today's digital age, a strong online presence is crucial. Most pet owners are active on social media, so maintaining a consistent presence on these platforms could do wonders for your pet care business.

Here are some ideas:

- Share pictures or videos of you interacting with pets
- Share testimonials from satisfied pet parents
- Post about ongoing promotions or new services
- Show behind-the-scenes glimpses of your pet care facilities

Ensure that your social media strategy is consistent, engaging, and representative of your brand.

6.7. Search Engine Optimization (SEO)

SEO is all about optimizing your online content to appear high in search engine results. When done correctly, SEO can increase visibility, boost organic website traffic, and lead to more inquiries.

Consider hiring an SEO specialist or learning the basics yourself to effectively use keywords, meta descriptions, and backlinks to improve your website's SEO.

6.8. Collaborating with Other Local Businesses

Partnering with local businesses such as pet stores or veterinary clinics can also be a hotbed of potential customers. These partnerships can lead to referrals, sponsored events, or even co-marketing efforts.

Consider offering exclusive discounts for customers referred by your business partners and agree on mutual promotional programs.

6.9. Tracking Performance

Once your marketing plan is in action, performance tracking is key to understand what's working and what needs adjustment.

Keep track of customer inquiries and how they found out about your services, monitor website and social media analytics, and consider conducting customer surveys to gauge your marketing effectiveness.

In conclusion, marketing your pet care services effectively requires time, effort, and strategic planning. However, the rewards of a robust marketing strategy are immeasurable, leading to increased awareness, new clients, and business growth. With a combination of careful planning and resilient execution, you will carve a niche for your pet business encouraging more paws through your door.

Chapter 7. Business Financials: Understanding Costs, Pricing and Profit Margins

Financial planning is a cornerstone of any successful business venture, including a pet care service. Precise understanding of your costs, pricing strategies, and profit margins is vital to ensure the profitability and continuity of your enterprise.

7.1. Startup and Operational Costs

Before starting, it's crucial to consider the various startup and operational costs you'll incur while setting up your pet sitting and dog walking business. Startup costs can include:

1. Initial Training: Whether you opt for online modules or in-person courses, professional training in pet care is essential.

2. Marketing Material: Business cards, flyers, a professional website, and online advertising all have associated costs.

3. Licensing and Insurance: You will need to register your business and buy liability insurance.

Operational costs will persist as your business continues. These include:

1. Continuous Training: To keep your skills and knowledge up-to-date.

2. Vehicle Costs: Petrol, car maintenance or public transport fees if you're traveling to client's homes.

3. Equipment: Leashes, treats, pet first aid kit, waste bags and other necessary items.

4. Marketing: Ongoing costs associated with advertising your services.

5. Administration: Accountant fees and software subscriptions for managing bookings and finances.

Consider all these costs when calculating the financial requirements of starting and maintaining your pet care business.

7.2. Pricing Your Services

Setting the right price for your services is a balancing act - charge too high and you risk losing potential clients; too low, and you won't cover your expenses or make a profit.

Research is vital. Find out what other pet care providers charge for similar services in your area. Use these figures to determine an average market price, and place your rates within that range.

Also, consider your unique selling proposition (USP) that may justify a higher price. This could be additional services, more flexible hours, or specialized qualifications.

Keep in mind packaging deals that bundle services together, offering an enticing discount to potential clients.

7.3. Calculating Profit Margins

Profit margins are crucial, as they depict your business's overall financial health. Profit margin is determined by deducting the cost of providing your service (your expenses) from your service price.

If you charge $20 for a dog walk session and your cost (transport, time, equipment, etc.) is about $5 per session, your profit is $15 per session. Therefore, your profit margin would be 75% ($15 profit / $20 price x 100).

A high-profit margin indicates a profitable and well-managed business, whereas a low-profit margin could suggest issues with pricing or cost controls.

7.4. Record Keeping and Financial Analysis

A well-managed set of books allows you to track expenses, income, and establish the financial health of your business. Consider investing in accounting software or hiring a bookkeeper or accountant.

Regular financial analysis helps you spot trends, address issues, and optimize your pricing structure. Consider monthly or quarterly reviews of your profit margins and look for ways to increase income or reduce costs.

Remember, the sustainability of your pet care business relies heavily on precise financial management. By understanding your costs, developing smart pricing strategies, and consistently monitoring profits, your pet care prowess will manifest not only in happy four-legged clients but also in a strong bottom line.

Chapter 8. Building a Stellar Reputation: Pet Safety and Care Standards

Your journey towards a successful pet care enterprise begins with a profound understanding of the primary responsibility at the center of it all: ensuring the safety and well-being of the animals entrusted to your care. Therefore, building a stellar reputation in this competitive industry requires adherence to high pet safety and care standards. In this segment, we shall explore the various factors that contribute to establishing superior care standards, starting from preparing yourself appropriately, understanding pet health and emergency situations, as well as shaping excellent customer service.

8.1. Preparing Yourself

To provide the highest standard of care to pets, you, as a pet sitter or a dog walker, must come prepared with an understanding of the job's demands. These include species-specific knowledge, the basics of pet health care, and being comfortable in dealing with emergency situations.

Species-specific Knowledge: Your clientele will invariably be diverse, hosting an array of pets each with unique needs and habits. It's imperative therefore, that you familiarize yourself with different types of pets, their behaviors, dietary needs, exercise characteristics, and suitable interaction styles.

Basic Pet Healthcare: Remember that a part of your job is to ensure the physical well-being of the pets. This necessitates a basic understanding of pet health, common health issues, first aid, and when it's time to involve a veterinarian.

Handling Emergencies: Emergencies are unpredictable. Equip yourself with the skillset and knowledge to handle potential emergencies effectively. This capability will set you apart as a reliable and responsible pet care provider.

8.2. Understanding Pet Health and Emergencies

A well-rounded pet care professional doesn't replace a veterinarian but plays a vital role in identifying health issues at initial stages, administering first aid, and ensuring pets get timely professional medical help when needed.

One key aspect here is knowing the norm for each pet under your care. Sometimes, changes in behavior, eating habits, or physiological signs can indicate an underlying health issue. For instance,

Changes in Appetite or Water Intake: Significant changes in a pet's eating or drinking patterns, especially if coupled with other symptoms like lethargy or drastic weight fluctuations, could be a red flag.

Unusual Behavior or Changes in Activity Levels: If a lively dog suddenly seems lethargic or a typically social cat begins hiding, it could indicate a potential health issue.

Bodily Signs: Look for unusual signs like difficulty in walking, irregular breathing, discoloration of gums, diarrhea, vomiting, or unusual discharge from eyes or nose.

In case of emergencies, be ready with basic first aid skills, know the location of the nearest emergency vet clinic, and have your client's pre-approval for emergency veterinary treatments.

8.3. Delivering Excellent Customer Service

While caring for pets is your primary role, liaising with pet owners is an equally important aspect of the business. Maintaining a transparent, reliable, and approachable relation strengthens trust and satisfaction, thereby enhancing your reputation.

Transparent Communication: Keep the pet owners informed about their pets' behavior, health, and well-being. Share regular updates through photographs, videos, or messages ensuring them that their pet is in excellent care.

Reliability: Be punctual and dependable in providing services as per the agreed schedule. Any change in plans should be adequately communicated and agreed upon with the pet owner.

Approachability: Be open and responsive to the pet owners' concerns, queries, or special requests. Remember, these animals are beloved members of their families, and clients will appreciate your keen attention to their idiosyncrasies.

A holistic understanding of pet safety and care is not only necessary for the well-being of the animals in your care, but also for establishing a reliable and reputable pet care business. Proper preparation, a robust understanding of pet health, competently handling emergencies, and prioritizing customer service form the backbone of establishing your pet sitting and dog walking business with panache and prowess. As you embrace these standards, not only will you carve a niche for your business, but you will also cultivate a safe, comfortable, and enriching environment for your furry clients, thereby making 'petrepreneurship' a truly rewarding endeavor.

Chapter 9. Nurturing Client Relationships: Customer Service in Pet Care

Pets are not just animals to their owners, they are precious members of their family. Therefore, pet owners look for pet care services that they can trust and that hold their pets' interests at heart. To capture that trust and develop a bond that ensures customer loyalty, superior customer service in your pet care business is paramount. Let's delve into how one can nurture and sustain healthy client relationships through enhanced customer service.

9.1. Understanding Your Clients

Understanding your clients and their pets is the first step towards delivering exceptional customer service. This entails getting to know their names, breeds, temperaments, specific preferences, and needs. Remembering these details and the personal aspect they bring to your service is not just a courtesy, but an opportunity to establish a bond and convey the message that every pet truly matters to you.

9.2. Empathy and Patience

As a pet care professional, empathizing with your clients is crucial. It's all about understanding their concerns, needs, or fears. Patience, too, is key. Dealing with pets isn't always easy, and patience will help you address customers' needs effectively, even in difficult situations.

9.3. Honesty and Transparency

It's vital to maintain transparency and honesty in all aspects of your service. This includes clear communication about pricing, services, and, most importantly, situations involving the pets in your care. This fosters trust and helps build long-term relationships.

9.4. Proactive Communication

Open and frequent communication aids in preempting issues and managing expectations effectively. This means providing regular updates, addressing concerns, and being reachable when clients need to reach you.

9.5. Going the Extra Mile

The extra steps you take to excite your clients can make a massive difference. This could involve sending pictures, videos, or updates of their pets during service hours or remembering special occasions, among others.

9.6. Training Your Team

Your team is the face of your customer service. Therefore, investing time and resources in training your team to offer excellent customer service can significantly boost your client relationships.

9.7. Feedback and Improvement

Lastly, it is crucial to actively seek feedback and continuously improve your services based on the responses. It shows clients their opinions matter, reinforcing their trust in your services.

In the following sections, you will find an in-depth exploration of these pillars of customer service in pet care.

9.8. Understand Your Clients: The Power of Personalization

Understanding the preferences of both pet and pet owner is crucial to delivering a personalized and superior customer service experience. By asking the right questions and taking notes during initial orientation or consultation sessions, one can gauge these preferences. Keeping a record of these interactions can help customize the service for every pet and owner, creating a personalized experience that drives loyalty.

9.9. Building Empathy into Your Pet Care Business: Connect on a Deeper Level

In your pet care business, empathy goes a long way in building stronger relationships with customers. By taking the time to understand and validate your clients' emotions and concerns, you can connect on a deeper level. Not only does empathy help in conflict resolution, but it also inspires a positive customer experience that eventually drives loyalty.

9.10. Honesty and Transparency: The Bedrock of Trust

One of the greatest determinants of customer trust is the level of honesty and transparency you demonstrate. Ensure you are honest about your services, especially under unexpected circumstances like pet injuries or accidents. Let your clients know what happened and tell them how you addressed the situation. This builds trust and communicates that you have their pets' best interests at heart.

9.11. Proactive Communication: Keeping Clients in the Loop

Keeping your clients updated about their pet's activities, sharing pictures or videos, informing them about any issues or changes in behavior, all fall into proactive communication. This instills a sense of security and trust among your clients and ensures that they feel connected, even when away from their pets.

9.12. Going Above and Beyond: Small Gestures, Big Impact

Go beyond the expectations of your clients by adding personal, thoughtful touches to your services. Celebrating a pet's birthday, remembering the pet owner's special occasions, or sending a thank-you note can make your clients feel valued and appreciated in a special way.

9.13. Training Your Team: Infusing Customer Service into Every Interaction

Train your team in the art of customer service, ensuring they understand its importance and know how to deliver it effectively. Regular training and refreshers on empathy, communication skills, conflict resolution, and customer engagement are critical in providing a high level of customer service.

9.14. Feedback and Improvement: The Cycle of Continuous Enhancement

Seeking feedback from customers gives them a sense of value and indicates your willingness to improve. Regularly ask for feedback, and use it to inform changes and improvements in your service. This ongoing cycle of feedback and enhancement reinforces your commitment to allowing your customers to shape their experience and fosters customer loyalty.

The customer service you provide can be the make-or-break factor for your pet care business. By knowing your client and their pets, being empathetic and patient, practicing honesty and transparency, communicating proactively, going the extra mile, equipping your team, and integrating feedback, you can carve out a distinguished place for your business in this industry.

Chapter 10. Mastering the Art of Team-Building and Management

Whether you're starting from scratch or expanding, a strong, well-coordinated team is a must for the success of your pet sitting and dog walking business. Let's begin by looking into the various aspects of team-building and management that you need to master for your business operations.

10.1. Identifying Roles and Responsibilities

Your pet care team will encompass a variety of roles - dog walkers, pet sitters, support staff, and more. Each role requires specific skills and personality traits. When clearly defined, these roles allow for smoother operations and help avoid confusion and conflict.

Dog walkers and pet sitters will need to love animals, of course, but they'll also need to be patient, reliable, and physically fit. Support staff, on the other hand, should have good organizational and interpersonal skills.

10.2. Recruitment Strategies

We all recognize the importance of hiring the right people. But how do you find them? Advertise vacancies on social media, job boards, in local newspapers and through word of mouth. When sifting through applications, look for people with a genuine love for animals as well as the skills to handle the technicalities of the job.

10.3. Training Your Team

New employees should undergo a comprehensive training program. Training will provide staff with the knowledge they need to perform their duties well and also ingrain your company's culture and values. The topics could range from pet first aid and handling different breeds, to customer service and using your business software.

10.4. Creating a Positive Work Culture

A positive work culture improves job satisfaction, reduces employee turnover and boosts productivity. Foster open communication, encouraging employees to share ideas and feedback. Arrange regular team-bonding activities, and give recognition where it's due.

10.5. Conflict Resolution Techniques

Given that your team will comprise of individuals with diverse viewpoints, conflicts can sometimes be inevitable. It's essential to swiftly and effectively resolve these issues to prevent harm to the work environment. Handle conflicts professionally, allowing every party involved to express their thoughts and feelings.

10.6. Employee Retention Tactics

A high turnover rate can negatively affect your business. Create a supportive work environment that people want to remain a part of. Some strategies could include offering competitive compensation packages, opportunities for professional growth and maintaining work-life balance.

10.7. Delegating Effectively

Delegation is a critical management skill that maximizes productivity. By entrusting responsibilities to your staff members, you're not only freeing up your time for higher-level tasks but also helping them develop their potential.

10.8. Performance Evaluations

Regular performance evaluations will help keep your team on track. Constructive feedback can inspire growth, reinforce good practices, and expose areas of improvement.

10.9. Encouraging Growth and Development

Supporting the professional growth and development of your employees will encourage employees to build a career with your company, not just work a job. Opportunities for ongoing training and development should be available to all employees.

As evident, creating and managing a successful team requires intent, effort, and strategic planning. However, seeing your business flourish thanks to a dedicated and harmonious team makes all the effort worth it. Implementing these strategies makes for efficient team management, ensuring your pet sitting and dog walking business is set up for long-term success.

Chapter 11. Planning for Future Growth: Strategies for Expansion and Sustainability

Successful growth and expansion of your pet care business hinge on strategic foresight and careful planning. Aiming for future growth involves not just broadening your client base, but also diversifying your services, refining your business model, and strengthening your financial footing. Cultivating sustainable practices will lead to a resilient, flexible, and adaptable organization that can weather market fluctuations and changes in client preferences.

11.1. Strategizing for Expansion

Rapt attention should be given to delineating a strategic plan for expansion. This involves setting measurable objectives, defining actionable steps, and emphasizing continuous monitoring and adjustment.

1. Define Your Goals: What degree of growth do you foresee for your business? Quantify your targets in terms of increased clients or services, expanded territories, and higher revenue. Consider the potential impact on your existing operations and resources.

2. Diversify Your Services: Broadening your offerings goes beyond offering more types of pet care services. Consider stepping into pet supplies, grooming, training, or even health-related services.

3. Explore Alliances and Affiliations: Forming partnerships with related businesses such as pet shops, vet clinics, and grooming salons can pave the way for cross-promotion and referral arrangements. This not only expands your reach but also adds a layer of trust through association.

4. Franchise Opportunities: If your pet care business model is unique and easily replicable, franchising can be a great way to grow and expand. You can provide the umbrella of your established brand while aspiring entrepreneurs manage the ground operations.

11.2. Developing a Business Continuity Plan

Business continuity planning ensures that your business operations can continue under adverse circumstances. It identifies potential threats and crafts handy strategies to mitigate the impacts.

1. Identify Key Business Functions: From caring for pets to maintaining client records, identify and list all the operational elements of your pet care business.

2. Risk Assessment: Identify potential risks that may disrupt your operations, like natural disasters, power outages, or staff shortages. Mitigate these risks and create contingency plans.

3. Disaster Recovery: Outline strategies for recovery in the event of catastrophe. This includes insurance coverages, data backup procedures, and alternative operational sites or work arrangements.

4. Regular Testing: Regularly reassess and amend your business continuity plan as required, ensuring it remains up-to-date and efficient.

11.3. Strengthening Financial Management

To accommodate future growth, your financial management needs to be rock solid. It's crucial to take steps to achieve financial resilience and stability.

1. Regular Budget Reviews: Regularly scrutinize your budgets and make necessary adjustments. Forecast your finances based on anticipated growth, new services, or planned investments.

2. Cash Flow Management: Monitor your cash flow vigilantly. Manage outflows and inflows effectively to ensure ample liquidity for emergencies and opportunities.

3. Investment in Technology: Consider growing your business by investing in management software, CRM systems, and online booking platforms.

4. Insurance: Robust insurance coverage is essential for safeguarding your finances. Seek appropriate insurance for professional liability, potential accidents, property damage, and worker's compensation.

11.4. Embracing Sustainable Business Practices

Sustainability has emerged as a crucial factor for any business. Ensure that your growth strategies and actions align with eco-friendly practices and societal construction.

1. Green Initiatives: From using biodegradable pet cleaning products to implementing energy-efficient practices, there are numerous ways to "go green".

2. Community Engagement: Engage with your local community. Sponsor local events, engage in charity work, or collaborate with local pet rescue organizations.

3. Ethical Practices: Ensure that all your practices are ethically sound. This could include humane treatment of animals, fair wages for employees, and honest dealings with clients.

In conclusion, planning for future growth means striking a balance between ambitious expansion strategies and sustainability plans. It involves fortifying your financial management while keeping the adaptability and resilience of your business in mind. While the journey towards growth and expansion might involve challenges, with the right strategies, you can thrive successfully in the pet care industry.